# Cornerstones of Freedom

# The Story of
# THE
# LITTLE
# BIGHORN

By R. Conrad Stein

Illustrated by David J. Catrow III

**P** CHILDRENS PRESS, CHICAGO

Library of Congress Cataloging in Publication Data

Stein, R. Conrad.
    The story of the Little Bighorn.

    (Cornerstones of freedom)
    Summary: Describes the bloody battle known as
"Custer's last stand," in which an army of Sioux
Indians led by Sitting Bull fought off an attack
by the United States cavalry, leaving no survivors
among the soldiers in Custer's command.
    1.  Little Big Horn, Battle of the, 1876—Juvenile
literature.  [1.  Little Big Horn, Battle of the, 1876.
2.  Sitting Bull, Dakota chief, 1831-1890.  3.  Custer,
George Armstrong, 1839-1876.  4.  Dakota Indians—Wars,
1876.  5.  Indians of North America—Wars]  I.  Catrow,
David J., ill.  II.  Title.  III.  Series.
E83.876.S73  1983       973.8'2       83-6594
ISBN 0-516-04663-2          AACR2

Never before had Plains Indians gathered in such numbers. Rows of tepees stretched along the Rosebud River. They formed a camp that measured five miles long and three miles wide. Nearly all the nations of the Sioux were there. So were the Cheyenne, the Arapaho, and the Blackfoot. In the past, some of those tribes had been enemies. But today they assembled peacefully. They had been summoned by the great Sioux chief Sitting Bull.

Sitting Bull was famous throughout the Indian world. He had once marched defiantly in front of soldiers' rifles as they blazed at an Indian war party. There he sat on the ground, filled his pipe, and lit it. Bullets whistled inches from his head. But the Sioux chief refused to budge until he had smoked a full bowl. As a high priest, Sitting Bull was known to have visions that could probe into the future. He often wandered into the hills and stayed there many days and nights. Those lonely vigils helped him to see a different world, a spirit world, where he could learn what the future held for his people.

He once claimed that when he walked barefoot on the soil, he could "hear the very heartbeat of the holy earth."

In the spring of 1876, Sitting Bull presided over the fifteen thousand men, women, and children who had gathered at the Rosebud. Four thousand warriors were ready to fight. The Sioux chief needed to call on his deepest spiritual powers. Hoping for a vision from the spirit world, he endured the agonizing ritual of the Sun Dance.

Just before daylight, Sitting Bull climbed to the top of a hill. He faced east, toward the rising sun. At his back stood a sacred pole. In a sing-song voice, he began to wail ancient prayers. While a circle of medicine men watched, another Sioux brave took out a knife. He cut a piece of skin from Sitting Bull's right wrist. Then he dug the knife into Sitting Bull's wrist once more. Again and again the knife slashed Sitting Bull's arm. Blood oozed from the wounds. The pain he felt must have been terrible. But Sitting Bull never flinched. He never even seemed to notice the steel blade gouging his skin. Instead, he continued praying in his monotonous, sing-song voice. When his right arm had been cut fifty times, Sitting Bull raised his left arm for the same punishing treatment. Ignoring pain was one of the ways used by a Sioux medicine man to reach the spirit world.

When blood was flowing freely from both arms, Sitting Bull began his dance. Facing the sun, he bobbed up and down on his toes. Shunning food and water, the Sioux chief danced all day and into the night. The hundred cuts on his arms blistered with pain, but he never ceased chanting his prayer-songs. Finally, after more than twenty-four hours of dancing, Sitting Bull collapsed. He had reached the state he hoped to achieve. The Indians called it "dying a passing death."

In his trancelike sleep, Sitting Bull had a remarkable vision. He saw hundreds of white soldiers and their horses falling upside down into the Indian camp. When he awoke, the Sioux chief told the medicine men of his vision. They spoke in hushed tones and then nodded in agreement. The dream could mean only one thing—the red man soon would win a stunning victory over the white man.

At the time Sitting Bull was suffering through the Sun Dance, another warrior was riding into Montana Territory. He, too, was a man with visions. He dreamed of becoming powerful in his government. Perhaps one day he would even become the

president of the United States. His name was George Armstrong Custer.

As a boy, Custer had longed to become a soldier. When he was eighteen, he entered the military academy at West Point. His performance as a student was dismal. Custer graduated with the worst grades of anyone in his class. At the time he graduated, the United States was locked in a bloody Civil War. Custer hurried off to the fighting front. There his fortunes skyrocketed. The young officer led his troops to glory in battles at Gettysburg, Cold Harbor, Yellow Tavern, and Five Forks. At twenty-three, he became the youngest general in the Union army. His bravery won him a chestful of medals and fame in both the North and the South.

After the Civil War, Custer stayed in the army. Like all officers who elected to remain in uniform, he accepted a peacetime demotion. He soon worked his way up to the rank of colonel, however. Transferred to the western frontier, Custer achieved even greater fame as an Indian fighter. Eastern newspapers printed stories of his glorious victories over the "savages." His popularity increased when he published an autobiography called *My Life on the Plains*. The book told of his battles with Indians.

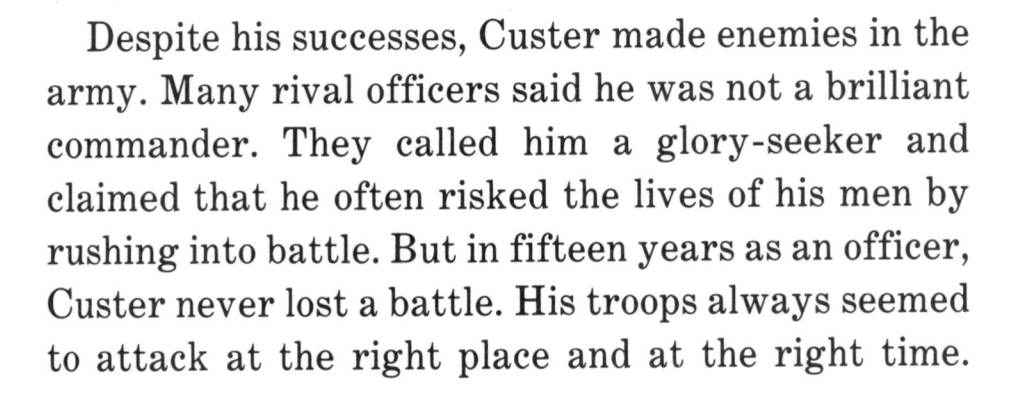

Despite his successes, Custer made enemies in the army. Many rival officers said he was not a brilliant commander. They called him a glory-seeker and claimed that he often risked the lives of his men by rushing into battle. But in fifteen years as an officer, Custer never lost a battle. His troops always seemed to attack at the right place and at the right time.

Custer's critics said his string of victories was due to what they called the "Custer luck." Like a winning card player, Custer always managed to draw the more-powerful hand. Over the years, the Custer luck became known and talked about by every soldier in the United States cavalry. Perhaps Custer believed in his marvelous luck, too. And perhaps he thought his luck would someday carry him to high office in Washington.

But first Custer had to battle Sitting Bull and an army of Plains Indians.

White invasion of Indian territory had started the war on the Plains. This was a long-standing problem on the American frontier. For decades, the Indians

had seen white men pushing onto their land. First came the white hunters who killed the buffalo. Then came the miners who fouled the streams. Finally, farmers strung barbed wire over land where Indians used to ride freely.

Wars broke out on the frontier. The white men had better weapons and usually had greater numbers. The Indians were forced to sign peace treaties with the government in Washington. The treaties confined the Indians to reservation lands. Many of the reservations were enormous, and the treaties promised the land to the Indians forever. One tribe was given their reservation for "as long as the rivers shall run and the grass shall grow." But even while the chiefs were signing that treaty, white settlers began moving onto their land.

In the 1870s, gold was discovered in the Black Hills. The Black Hills were sacred to the Indian people of the Great Plains. The Indians believed the land to be the resting place of the souls of their ancestors. A treaty signed by the government in Washington guaranteed that the Black Hills would be Indian land forever. Suddenly this holy ground swarmed with white gold-seekers. The furious Indians attacked the mining camps. The government sent troops, and a bloody war began.

Into this war on the Great Plains came the famous Indian fighter George Armstrong Custer.

Riding with Custer were several Indian scouts. His most trusted Indian advisor was an Arikara chief named Bloody Knife. Chief Bloody Knife studied the thousands of hoofprints and acres of chewed-up grass along the Rosebud riverbank. These signs meant that an immense band of Sioux had camped there recently.

Bloody Knife reported his findings to Custer. The colonel pondered what to do. He commanded about six hundred men. According to his scout, the Sioux force could number in the thousands. The Indian

trail led away from the Rosebud toward some high ground. Behind that high ground flowed a river the Indians called the Greasy Grass. The white men called it the Little Bighorn.

Custer mounted his horse, pointed toward the Little Bighorn, and gave the command "Forward, ho!"

For the next one hundred years, historians would argue about why Custer chose to attack even though he must have known he would be woefully outnumbered. Another large cavalry unit probed the hills near him. Custer's orders were to locate the Sioux camp and, together with that other unit, attack it. So why did Custer decide to attack the Sioux with only his six hundred men? Some historians believe that Custer wanted to win a smashing victory and see his name splashed in the newspaper headlines in the east. Others point out that Custer had always been a brave and aggressive leader. It was only natural for him to try to surprise his enemy by striking the first blow. Whatever his reasons, Custer's decision led to tragedy for his regiment and to a century of debate for historians.

Obediently, the men of the Seventh Cavalry followed their colonel toward the Little Bighorn Valley. Perhaps the men felt that their commander's luck would once again pull them through the coming battle. Many of those troops noticed their leader's new haircut. For year's Custer's trademark had been the long locks of yellow hair that flowed behind him as he raced his horse. The Indians called the colonel Yellow Hair. But at his wife's request, Custer got a short haircut just a few days before he entered this campaign. Later, some soldiers would think of the Bible story of Samson. Samson of old had the strength of one hundred men. But his strength was mysteriously linked to his long hair. When Samson's hair was cut short, his astonishing strength vanished. Some cavalry troops would soon wonder if Custer's remarkable good luck was not also, somehow, linked to his long yellow hair.

At the Little Bighorn Valley, Custer divided his forces. He sent three companies under Captain Benteen to scout his left flank. Three more companies under Major Marcus Reno rode through the valley from the south. Custer then rode over the highland with five companies to enter the valley from the north. By dividing his forces, Custer hoped to surround his enemy. However, he succeeded only in compounding his mistake. Attacking the Indians with such a small force was Custer's first mistake. Splitting that force into even smaller units was his second.

Because Custer split his forces, two separate battles were fought on the Little Bighorn River. One battle raged for two days, and one fourth of a cavalry unit was killed or wounded. The other battle

lasted a matter of minutes, and no cavalry soldier survived.

Major Reno's troops made the first contact with the Sioux. Rounding a bend in the river, the major discovered about thirty Indians. Most were boys who stood guard over a herd of horses. Following Custer's order, Reno's 130 men galloped over the shallow waters to attack. Suddenly the cavalry men saw a boiling cloud of dust rolling off the riverbank. Indian braves on horseback—perhaps a thousand of them—thundered toward the soldiers. At first the men tried to stand and fight. But Reno then ordered them to fall back. The soldiers wheeled about on their horses and scrambled toward a tree-covered hill. The retreat quickly became a rout.

One of the survivors of this battle was a captain named Edward S. Godfrey. In a magazine article written years later, the captain said, "Reno gave orders to those near him to mount and get to the bluff. . . . Owing to the noise of the firing, many did not know of the order until too late." The hill the men climbed was covered with boulders and ran practically straight up. But, as Godfrey wrote, "It was surprising to see what steep inclines men and horses clambered up under the excitement of danger."

Indian survivors also left descriptions of Reno's retreat. A Sioux named Henry Oscar One Bull said, "the soldiers were mixed up. Some got off their horses and began firing as we rode in. Others stayed mounted. Two soldiers couldn't hold their horses in all the excitement. The horses bolted, carrying their riders right into our warriors. Those soldiers didn't last long." A Cheyenne chief named Two Moon remembered, "The air was full of smoke and dust. I saw the soldiers drop back and fall into the riverbed like buffalo fleeing. They had no time for a crossing. The Sioux chased them up the hill."

At the top of the hill, the cavalry men crouched behind trees and fired at the Sioux. Dozens of horses were killed. Some soldiers used the bodies of their horses to shield themselves from Indian arrows and bullets. Others dug trenches in the rock-covered ground. They knew they were in for a long, desperate struggle.

From a distance, Sitting Bull watched the battle. The Sioux chief did not fight in the front ranks that day. Instead, he served as the religious leader and organizer of the Plains Indians. In camp, he chanted prayers for his warriors. One of those warriors was an Oglala Sioux chief named Crazy Horse.

Crazy Horse was a ferocious fighter and a brilliant leader of horsemen. Just eight days earlier he had led a huge war party to victory over a cavalry unit at the Rosebud River. At the northern end of the valley, Crazy Horse commanded almost two thousand braves. He and his men were eager to meet the next group of white soldiers foolish enough to enter the valley of the Little Bighorn.

The Indians who fought under Crazy Horse had a strange assortment of arms. Many fought with what was called a coup stick. It was a long pole used to strike or spear enemy horsemen. Other Indians had rifles. They were outdated single-shot weapons. Most of the Plains Indians were armed with trusted

bows and arrows. For three thousand years warriors throughout the world had fought with bows and arrows. This would be the last major battle in world history in which the winning side was armed primarily with bows and arrows.

In the highland, Custer and his 230 men saw the enormous Sioux camp. Countless tepees stood along the riverbank. Surely this was history's largest gathering of Plains Indians. Perhaps in one frightening instant Custer realized his mistake in tackling such a gigantic force. Students of history will always wonder if Custer entered this battle with his usual feeling of supreme confidence. Or did he ride into the valley with a single question burning in his mind—my God, what have I done?

At the riverbank, Custer and his men were quickly surrounded. Led by the hard-riding Crazy Horse, the massed braves poured in on the soldiers from every direction. The valley echoed with shrill Indian war whoops, the cracking of rifles, the neighing of terrified horses, and the dreadful screams of wounded and dying men.

From the camp, Sitting Bull looked on as a cloud of dust covered the battle scene. He did not need to watch this battle to know what the outcome would be. He had seen it in his vision during the Sun Dance.

No white soldier in the five companies commanded by Custer lived to tell his story of the fight. Years later, Indian braves were interviewed by writers. They gave vivid descriptions. A warrior named Low Dog remembered, "I called to my men, 'This is a good day to die: follow me.' As we rushed upon them, the white soldiers dismounted to fire, but they did a very poor job shooting. They held their horse reins in one arm while they were shooting, but their horses were so frightened that they pulled the men all around. A great many of their shots went up in the air and did us no harm. The white soldiers stood their ground bravely and none of them made an attempt to get away."

A Sioux named Dewey Beard was called away from the fighting against Major Reno and dashed four miles up the river to do battle against Custer. He said, "This new battle was a turmoil of dust and warriors and soldiers, with bullets whining and arrows hissing all around. Sometimes a bugle would sound and the shooting would get louder. Some of the soldiers were firing pistols at close range. Our knives and war clubs flashed in the sun. I could hear bullets whiz past my ear. But I kept going and shouting, 'It's a good day to die!' so that everyone who heard would know I was not afraid of being killed in battle."

It is not certain how Custer himself was finally brought down. A Sioux warrior named White Bull believed he was the slayer. Curiously, White Bull was Sitting Bull's nephew. He told of a hand-to-hand struggle with a single white soldier. "I charged in. A tall, well-built soldier with yellow hair and

mustache saw me coming and tried to bluff me, aiming his rifle at me. But when I rushed him he threw his rifle at me without shooting. I dodged it. We grabbed each other and wrestled there in dust and smoke. It was like fighting in a fog. This soldier was very strong and brave.... Finally I broke free. He drew his pistol. I wrenched it out of his hand and struck him with it three or four times on the head, knocked him over, shot him in the head, and then fired at his heart."

On June 25, 1876, the Custer luck vanished like a puff of gunsmoke. All 230 men in Custer's immediate command were killed. According to Indian reports, the battle was over in less than half an hour.

To the south, Major Reno had been joined on the hill by the three companies under Captain Benteen. Those men of the Seventh Cavalry fought the Indians in a battle that dragged on for two days. Fifty of their number died in the fighting. Still they were lucky. They were attacked near a hill that they could climb and defend. Custer, their suddenly luckless commander, had been caught on open ground.

Finally, Reno and Benteen were joined by a large cavalry unit that rode in from the south. The Indians were forced to retreat. That same large cavalry unit had intended to join Custer in the attack on the Indian camp. Had Custer waited, he might have averted tragedy.

The Little Bighorn battle was fought the year Americans celebrated their one hundredth birthday. The mood of the country was confident. Hopeful farmers streamed to what seemed to be endless empty land in the west. Few of those farmers cared that the "empty" land had been the Indians' home for centuries. Most American people believed the

Indians to be Godless savages who did not deserve the fine land that lay to the west.

A large part of the people's attitude toward the Indians had been molded by stories they read in newspapers and books. Those stories portrayed the Indians as being treacherous and cruel. The New York *Herald* of July 13, 1876, described the Indian braves at Little Bighorn as "those wild swarming horsemen circling along the heights like shrieking vultures waiting for the moment to sweep down and finish the bloody tale." A newspaper story dated July 12 claimed that an Indian named Rain-in-the-Face had killed Custer. "Rain-in-the-Face cut the heart from Colonel Custer's body and held a grand war dance around it."

Nearly every newspaper in the country claimed the battle had been an attack *by* the Sioux *on* the cavalry. Actually, Custer and his men were attacking the Sioux camp. In that camp were thousands of women and children. At least one newspaperman, however, pleaded for fairness in treatment of the Little Bighorn battle. Writing in the Boston *Transcript,* editor Wendell Phillips asked, "What kind of war is it where, if we kill the enemy it is death; if he kills us it is massacre?"

Still, most Americans chose to believe the more-sensational stories about events on the Little Bighorn. After the battle, they demanded that more soldiers be sent west to deal with the "savages."

The army quickly sent more soldiers to the frontier. They also began an investigation of the battle. The investigation revealed Custer's two major mistakes—attacking without waiting for reinforcements and dividing his forces. During the investigation, a general named Samuel Sturgis said of Custer, [He] "was a brave man, but also a very selfish man. He was insanely ambitious of glory... and had no regard for the soldiers under him."

Dozens of books and stories soon were written about the Little Bighorn battle. The battle also inspired artists to paint scenes of it. It is estimated that nine hundred different artists have painted pictures of Custer's desperate fight on the riverbank. Of course, no artist witnessed the battle. So most of the pictures are highly fictionalized. Like the books and stories, they show brave, clean-cut cavalry men fighting painted savages. The most popular painting of the battle was commissioned by the Anheuser Busch beer company. It shows Custer with a sword drawn over his head about to slay a Sioux brave. The beer company had 150,000 lithograph copies of this painting printed. The copies were pasted on the walls of saloons and beer halls across the nation. The famous painting was called "Custer's Last Stand."

Actually, the Battle of the Little Bighorn could be considered the Plains Indians' last stand. They had won an important victory, but never again would they command such power. Shortly after the battle, the Sioux broke into smaller camps in order to hunt buffalo. The smaller lodges were easy prey for patroling cavalry troops. In the fall of 1876, soldiers under the command of General Crook raided thirty-seven Indian camps. Because of the loss of the Seventh Cavalry, the soldiers burned for revenge. Their victims included old people, children, and women.

Sitting Bull was forced to flee to Canada with a small band of followers. In his absence, other chiefs signed a peace treaty with a representative of the government in Washington. The treaty pushed the Plains Indians onto a new, smaller reservation. Worst of all, the Sioux lost the Black Hills—that sacred land that had been promised to them forever.

Gold-seekers soon flocked to the Black Hills. They were followed by ranchers, farmers, and men who hammered steel railroad tracks into wooden ties.

Now and then, these busy newcomers looked up from their work and saw bands of Indians standing motionless and gazing at the horizon. Most of them were old men and women who seemed to be lost in their dreams.

Why had those old people returned to the Black Hills? Many had come to try to hear the whispers of their ancestors, whose souls they believed rested in this eternal land. Others had come to remember the hundreds of years when Indian people rode freely over the Great Plains. And a few of the old people had come to the Black Hills to die. No government in Washington could prevent them from doing that, at least.

## About the Author

R. Conrad Stein was born and grew up in Chicago. He enlisted in the Marine Corps at the age of eighteen, and served for three years. He then attended the University of Illinois, where he received a Bachelor's Degree in history. He later studied in Mexico and earned a Master of Fine Arts degree from the University of Guanajuato.

The study of history is Mr. Stein's hobby. Since he finds it to be an exciting subject, he tries to bring the excitement of history to his readers. He is the author of many other books, articles, and short stories written for young people.

Mr. Stein is married to Deborah Kent, who is also a writer of books for young readers.

## About the Artist

David J. Catrow III was born in Virginia and grew up in Hudson, Ohio. He spent three years in the United States Navy as a hospital corpsman then subsequently attended Kent State University, where he majored in biology. He is a self-taught illustrator. Mr. Catrow currently lives in Hudson, Ohio with his wife Deborah Ann and daughter Hillary Elizabeth. The artist would like to thank Deborah for her constant support and inspiration.